the power of
christian
friendship

Dr. Freddy B. Wilson
& Joyce A. Armster

the power of

christian

friendship

WILSONET ENTERPRISES

friendships

This message is for a new day and time for Christians. We would like to talk about the power of Christian friendship. Christian friends recently spoke to each other after many years. The friends had known each other for almost thirteen years, but each moved away. It was just great for them as they rekindled old times. Most of the time they talked about what the Lord can do. God is just that good, because you can share your blessing with a friend and inspire that friend to trust in the Lord, and let the Lord guide you, no matter how tough things seem at this time.

Many Christians have espoused the idea that the Lord is all a person needs. This, by far, is true; however, God never intended for us to be alone or function as an island. The Bible has provided many examples that indicate that God meant for us to have earthly friends, but most of all, he wants us to be friends with him! God's Word tells us that a friend sticks closer than a brother, and that in order for one to be a friend, one must show themselves friendly (Proverbs 18:24).

> So the LORD spoke to Moses face to face, as a man speaks to his friend. And he would return to the camp, but his servant Joshua the son of Nun, a young man, did not depart from the tabernacle. Then Moses said to the LORD, "See, You say to me, 'Bring up this people.' But You have not let me know whom You will send with me. Yet You have said, 'I know you by name, and you have also found grace in My sight.'"
>
> Exodus 33:11-12 (NKJV)

It is difficult to find true Christian friendship in this often phony, temporary world. For whatever reason, some Christians find it difficult to see another brother or sister progress, and some can think of nothing better than to see another brother or sister going through hard times. However, a genuine Christian friendship involves a shared sense of caring and concern, a desire to see one another grow and develop, and a hope for each other to succeed in all aspects of life. Faithfulness and loyalty are keys to true friendship.

1 Samuel 20 is about a covenant friendship in God's name. 1 Samuel 20 focuses on the friendship of David and Jonathan. These two men truly cared for each other and had great trust and confidence in one another. David was running for his life from Jon-

athan's father, Saul. Jonathan recognized that David was innocent. Because of the true friendship they shared, David survived Saul's assassination attempts and went on to become one of Israel's greatest kings.

> So Hushai, David's friend, went into the city. And Absalom came into Jerusalem. When David was a little past the top *of the mountain,* there was Ziba the servant of Mephibosheth, who met him with a couple of saddled donkeys, and on them two hundred *loaves* of bread, one hundred clusters of raisins, one hundred summer fruits, and a skin of wine.
>
> 2 Samuel 15:37-16:1 (NKJV)

> Meanwhile, Absalom and all the people, the men of Israel, came to Jerusalem; and Ahithophel *was* with him. And so it was, when Hushai the Archite, David's friend, came to Absalom, that Hushai said to Absalom, "*Long* live the king! *Long* live the king!" So Absalom said to Hushai, "*Is* this your loyalty to your friend? Why did you not go with your friend?" And Hushai said to Absalom, "No, but whom the LORD and this people and all the men of Israel choose, his I will be, and with him I will remain."
>
> 2 Samuel 16:15-18 (NKJV)

One thing that is good about special Christian friendships is that we can laugh and talk about anything and cover different subjects, and not just talk about the Lord. Christians need to realize is that not every conversation you have with someone has to be about the Lord, but people you talk to do need to know where you stand with the Lord. This way there is no question about your Christianity. All friendships should be uplifting. Real friendships look at the heart, not just the "packaging." Genuine friendship loves for love's sake, not just for what it can get in return. True friendship is both challenging and exciting. It risks, it overlooks faults, and it loves unconditionally; but it also involves being truthful, even though it may hurt. Genuine friendship, also called "agape" love, comes from the Lord. The Bible discusses this.

> What strength do I have, that I should hope? And what *is* my end, that I should prolong my life? *Is* my strength the strength of stones? Or is my flesh bronze? *Is* my help not within me? And is success driven from me? To him who is afflicted, kindness *should be shown* by his friend, Even though he forsakes the fear of the Almighty.
>
> Job 6:11-14 (NKJV)

Speaking to others about the Lord in the workplace can be difficult. Federal government employee rules do not allow management to proselytize to subordinates. Rules limit management as to what they can say concerning "religion." Nevertheless, sometimes you have to take a chance, but not necessarily to try to convert someone to Christianity. You should let them know how good God is and that he can help them in their situations. Most people who work around you should already be able tell that you are a Christian without your having to say so. They may hear you speak about the Lord, and may not want to hear it at first. Allow your witnessing to sink in without your pushing and they may want to hear what you have to say. They might have already paid close attention to what you have been saying.

God puts people into your life to help you. Moreover, it is wonderful when he send you a Christian friend, because a good friend is hard to come by nowadays. Whatever you promise to do, you should do it; because God said it is better not make a vow, than to make one and not keep it. We have to give in account for every word that proceeded out of our mouth, and the laws of reaping and sowing still apply even today.

> A man *who has* friends must himself be friendly,
> but there is a friend *who* sticks closer than a
> brother. Better *is* the poor who walks in his integ-
> rity than *one who is* perverse in his lips, and is a
> fool.
>
> Proverbs 18:24-19:1 (NKJV)

Sometimes being a good Christian friend does not
necessarily mean having to preach to your friends all
the time, or to have worship every time you talk. It
could mean just being there for a friend and sticking
to your word. For example, if you tell a friend you will
help them move, then you should make every effort to
help them move. If you tell someone you will be there
when he or she needs you, then by golly, when he or
she calls on you, you should be willing to go.

> LORD, who may abide in Your tabernacle? Who
> may dwell in Your holy hill? He who walks
> uprightly, and works righteousness, and speaks the
> truth in his heart; He *who* does not backbite with
> his tongue, nor does evil to his neighbor, nor does
> he take up a reproach against his friend; In whose
> eyes a vile person is despised, but he honors those
> who fear the LORD; he *who* swears to his own hurt
> and does not change.
>
> Psalms 15:1-4 (NKJV)

Sometimes being a Christian will cause you to lose some people you once considered good friends. John P. Kee sings in one of his songs that when you turn your life over to the Lord, you will lose some of your old relationships, for those relationships will not last. That is not necessarily a bad thing, for you do not want anyone hindering your witnessing and serving the Lord. In addition, any person that leaves you probably was not a good friend to begin with. You should never lower your standards or lower your servitude to the Lord because you want to keep a certain friend. The Bible says if you forget about the Lord, the Lord will forget about you. You should always know the Lord and know he can help you, and know that he is your God.

It is harder to make amends with an offended friend than to capture a fortified city. Arguments separate friends like a gate locked with iron bars, especially when you make a choice to serve the Lord. When we have offended a true friend—whether by breaking a trust or by speaking the truth with love—we risk losing that friendship. We must be careful not to break the trust, but when not speaking the truth will cause greater hurt in our friend's life, we must be willing to sacrifice our needs for those of our friend.

All who hate me whisper together against me; Against me they devise my hurt. "An evil disease," they say, "clings to him. And *now* that he lies down, he will rise up no more." ⁹ Even my own familiar friend in whom I trusted, who ate my bread, has lifted up *his* heel against me.

Psalms 41:7-9 (NKJV)

When the thought of a certain friend you have not talked to in a while comes to mind out of nowhere, it might be the Lord talking to you. You need to try your best to stop what you are doing and call that friend. That friend might be calling on to the Lord at that time, and your call might make a difference and let them know God does exist and he is listening to their prayers. You should make yourself available to sharpen your Christian friend. As iron sharpens iron, So a man sharpens the countenance of his friend (Proverbs 27:17, NKJV).

Having a good friend is almost like having a good marriage; they both require work. Of course, marriage takes more work than a friendship. Nevertheless, having a friendship takes work by keeping in touch with one another and being open and honest with one another. You may not live in the same city or area, but you should call that friend occasionally; for good friends are hard to find. You should cherish the friendship you do have.

> You are snared by the words of your mouth; You are taken by the words of your mouth. So do this, my son, and deliver yourself; for you have come into the hand of your friend: Go and humble yourself; plead with your friend. Give no sleep to your eyes, nor slumber to your eyelids. Deliver yourself like a gazelle from the hand *of the hunter*, And like a bird from the hand of the fowler.
>
> Proverbs 6:2-5 (NKJV)

There is an expression found in different songs that says no one can hurt you like a close friend or family member, so keeping the right friends is important. When those people that you thought were your friends are intentionally attacking you, it is time for you to realize the need to let those friends go. In the meantime, being a good Christian friend, you should be able to tell those persons honestly what they did to offend you. Sometimes forgiveness can come from people who were ignorant that they were hurting you. If you see that those friends were intentionally trying to hurt you, just pray to God and place the matter in his hands. No Christian should be a fool to another person. When the Bible says to turn the other cheek, it does not mean to turn your cheek to be hit there as well.

> A friend loves at all times, And a brother is born for adversity. A man devoid of understanding shakes hands in a pledge, *and* becomes surety for his friend. He who loves transgression loves strife, and he who exalts his gate seeks destruction. He who has a deceitful heart finds no good, and he who has a perverse tongue falls into evil.
>
> Proverbs 17:17-20 (NKJV)

Christian friendships are important today, because Christians should turn to other wise and like-minded people for advice. This could include just having someone to sound off to. Worldly people won't understand the perplexity of what Christians are dealing with as they are trying to live their lives right. The power of Christian friendship will enable us to move from one level to another and still maintain a strong friendship.

> So He told a parable to those who were invited, when He noted how they chose the best places, saying to them: "When you are invited by anyone to a wedding feast, do not sit down in the best

place, lest one more honorable than you be invited by him; and he who invited you and him come and say to you, 'Give place to this man,' and then you begin with shame to take the lowest place. But when you are invited, go and sit down in the lowest place, so that when he who invited you comes he may say to you, 'Friend, go up higher.' Then you will have glory in the presence of those who sit at the table with you. For whoever exalts himself will be humbled, and he who humbles himself will be exalted."

Luke 14:7-11 (NKJV)

One of the prevailing myths out there is that men and women cannot be friends without having a sexual relationship. You will find some pastors at churches say that married women cannot have a friendship with a male outside of her husband. We beg to differ in that opinion. A spouse should be a *best* friend, but does not have to be the *only* friend. A non-intimate external relationship can actually assist the person in maintaining their value in the relationship with their spouse. That friend of the opposite gender can give that person a perspective of their mate that they could not otherwise understand themselves. For example, a married man could talk to a Christian female friend about a problem. The friend could enlighten the man on how to deal with and approach his wife. We do agree that there should not be too much information shared to avoid being manipulated by a weak friend.

An example of the positive side of this sort of friendship is when a married couple in a military family has an external male friend. This sort of friendship is essential during times of short tours or deployments where the female may not be located near family during her husband's absence. The Christian female should be able to call on the Christian friend should she need help around the house, or other needs that arise. She should be able to contact him for just a simple sanity check in times of need. The deployed husband should be able to feel confident that his friend is helping his family and have no worries of an inappropriate relationship occurring during his absence.

> Adulterers and adulteresses! Do you not know that friendship with the world is enmity with God? Whoever therefore wants to be a friend of the world makes himself an enemy of God. Or do you think that the Scripture says in vain, "The Spirit who dwells in us yearns jealously"?
>
> James 4:4-5 (NKJV)

Everyone needs friends, including Christians. This includes some pastors of our churches who probably do not have anyone in their congregation to turn to as a friend when they are having trouble with things in their lives. One example that we can provide is that at one point in Dr. Wilson's marriage, he was dealing with some serious problems with his wife. This was coming from a strong Christian who believed in God and had prayed about the situation. He felt he was coming to the end of his rope with his wife; however, a good friend of his, a single Christian female, talked to him about his situation and always encouraged him to pray. She finally told him that he needed to stick to his marriage and pray that God reveals to his wife what she was doing to their relationship. Dr. Wilson's friend explained that no one is perfect and that he should take an overall look at the situation. The advice proved to be sound.

Through this experience, Dr. Wilson was able to remain strong in his relationship and turn to God to help him in dealing with his wife. Things turned out well! The value behind talking to a Christian friend, rather than a worldly friend, is that a Christian friend can help you see the right perspective in dealing with your problem. Typically, that friend can help you with prayer about your situation. The Bible says that where two or more are gathered, God is there. Therefore, that Christian friend could be that second person that helps you pray through your situation. We also need to have another person to sound off to sometimes. We know most of us say we speak to the Lord; but we sometimes need to have another person to talk with.

When praying for solutions when dealing with others, we can start by forgiving. Accept the fact that people will not change unless God changes them. We all have some good and bad in us. Stop looking at the negative and focus on the positive; then figure out what you have contributed to cause the situation to go sour. It is amazing that we can always see the bad in others, but find it hard to turn the mirror around and take a good look at ourselves. There is no greater example than the love God has for us. His love is so great that he gave his only begotten Son, Jesus Christ, in order that our friendship with God might be restored. God did that in spite of the fact that we have offended him deeply. We have disobeyed God's commands, turned our backs on him, and followed our own path, yet he forgave us. God knows that we are not perfect and that we are still under his construction.

There is an expression that says, "God is good, all the time; all the time, God is good." That also applies with God putting others in our lives with whom we can be friends. Christians have other things they can do in their lives other than going to church. There are ball games, movies, having dinner, attending cookouts, and many other things we can do together as friends. Christians should be able to simply enjoy what God places on earth for us to enjoy. A good Christian friend can join you in just having fun without committing sin or being out committing crimes.

> And the Scripture was fulfilled which says, *"Abraham believed God, and it was accounted to him for righteousness."* And he was called the friend of God. You see then that a man is justified by works, and not by faith only.
>
> James 2:23-24 (NKJV)

There are times in Christian friendship, especially between men and women, where temptation can prevail. Of particular note is when one or both of the parties are married to someone else. The friends can find themselves attracted to one another. If both Christians are devoted to their vows to the Lord, then they can acknowledge the situation, deal with it, and get away from any temptation there might be. It is better for the friends to acknowledge the problem and honestly talk about the situation with that friend. Maybe if you are good enough friends, you can work through those problems without it interfering with the relationship with the husband, wife, boyfriend, or girlfriend of the committed friend.

> Faithful *are* the wounds of a friend, but the kisses of an enemy *are* deceitful. A satisfied soul loathes the honeycomb, but to a hungry soul every bitter thing *is* sweet. Like a bird that wanders from its nest *Is* a man who wanders from his place. Ointment and perfume delight the heart, and the sweetness of a man's friend *gives delight* by hearty counsel. Do not forsake your own friend or your father's friend, nor go to your brother's house in the day of your calamity; better *is* a neighbor nearby than a brother far away.
>
> Proverbs 27:6-10 (NKJV)

Another example: Dr. Wilson has been married to his wife for twenty-one years; they have been through their difficulties, and having Christian friends to talk along the way was good. Dr. Wilson's having good Christian friends to talk to has really made a difference. Many of those Christian friends have been women. Dr. Wilson felt the women were much easier to talk with. They have been there for him without adding any temptation. One example is that Dr. Wilson had a long-term friendship with the co-author of this book, Joyce Armster, before he met his wife. He was able to talk about anything to this friend. Some say a man should be able to talk to his wife about everything. This is not always possible, especially if you are dealing with a person that does not talk to you when they are angry. Dr. Wilson's wife knew this person to be his friend and did not have a problem with her. At one point in his career, Dr. Wilson moved his family to Georgia from Virginia. He moved his family into a home in Fayetteville, Georgia, but still had a job and a house to sell in Williamsburg, Virginia. After he moved his family, Dr. Wilson had nowhere to go other than an empty house with no furniture or appliances. Dr. Wilson's wife suggested he live temporarily with his female Christian friend, Joyce Armster, who lived in Hampton, Virginia, while he awaited the Lord to bless them to sell their old home and provide a new job in Georgia. That worked out well, for Dr. Wilson was able to talk to this friend about many things he was dealing with. This friend was able to help him pray over certain situations, and that friend was there for him when things got tough.

Oddly enough, that friend decided to move to the Atlanta area a year later and stayed with the Wilsons during her house-hunting trip. There were no incidents where relationships with the friend or Dr. Wilson's wife were in jeopardy. When Joyce Armster later returned to the Atlanta area to close on her house, she intended to stay with the Wilsons for two days. The house closing fell through and Joyce ended up staying about two weeks. They were able to pray together that things would turn around so she could close on the house regardless of the new problems. Joyce was comforted knowing she and her daughter had a safe place to stay. This is where true friendship, especially Christian friendship, has its benefits.

Having a good Christian friend is beneficial to single persons as well, whether the friend is married or single. Having sincere conversations with that person will help steer you straight in your life when things become difficult and you need someone with whom to talk. When you need someone to help you move, that person can be there for you. When you need someone to help you figure out something you are dealing with, that person can be there. Having a Christian friendship adds an extra level of comfort, for that person will not present a worldly perspective to issues you discuss.

attitude

Your attitude can make a difference in a friendship. This applies to the friendship you should have with your spouse. Great marriages come out of great friendships. It is better to have a faithful companion that shares your faith. Do not do anything in life that does not require faith. Sometimes we do things or seek friends to have a sense of security. Only the insecure strive for security. You should seek the Lord for your security and all else will fall into place. Life can send you on a journey of three different ships. Past information has shown that there is a good ship, a bad ship, but the best thing is friendship.

> A friend loves at all times, and a brother is born
> for adversity.
>
> Proverbs 17:17 (NKJV)

Do not let your life be a continual struggle, and do not do things you should not. Stop trying to be something you are not. You should strive to be yourself! If you are struggling with your self-image, look to Christ as to what you should be. If there are problem areas in your personality or personal life, seek help or self-help initiatives to resolve them. No person is perfect, and we all have our flaws. Gain some wisdom in life by trying to be understanding. Avoid distractions from God in any relationship. Some good friendships will help you grow in the Lord, while bad ones will bring you down.

> Wealth makes many friends, but the poor is sepa-
> rated from his friend. A false witness will not go
> unpunished, and *he who* speaks lies will not escape.
> Many entreat the favor of the nobility, and every
> man *is* a friend to one who gives gifts. All the
> brothers of the poor hate him; How much more do
> his friends go far from him! He may pursue *them*
> *with* words, *yet* they abandon *him*. He who gets
> wisdom loves his own soul; He who keeps under-
> standing will find good.
>
> Proverbs 19:4-8 (NKJV)

You should determine the veracity of your friendships. This does not mean you should put friends to a test; but you do have to determine if being your friend has any ulterior motives. Some folks will love you for what you have or what you represent, while others will love you based on what they think you can do for them.

> If your brother, the son of your mother, your son or your daughter, the wife of your bosom, or your friend who is as your own soul, secretly entices you, saying, "Let us go and serve other gods," which you have not known, neither you nor your fathers, of the gods of the people which *are* all around you, near to you or far off from you, from *one* end of the earth to the *other* end of the earth, you shall not consent to him or listen to him, nor shall your eye pity him, nor shall you spare him or conceal him.
>
> Deuteronomy 13:6-8 (NKJV)

You should build on your victories in life and share them with Christian friends. When God gives you a vision or insight into a future journey, you cannot share that with just anyone. Most Christian friends will understand God-given visions, but not all will understand. You just have a better chance that a Christian friend will understand before a worldly person would.

Stop taking journeys into your past. It is okay to share old times with your friends, but do not dwell on them. If you spend too much time in the past, your sight of the future will be dim. Let God guide your future and give you discernment as to who should be your friends. Be positive and know that you are blessed!

choices

You have to make wise choices of friends and in life. Most of our dysfunction is a result of poor choices. God gives you a choice, and that choice has consequences. Making the right choices will get you far in life in God's abundance. Sometimes you have to take risks to get unstuck in life. However, you must maintain your integrity. Some people, including Christians, think the way to being blessed is to cheat some system to obtain benefits that you do not ordinarily qualify for. This is a poor way to receive a blessing! God can bless you regardless of your situation. You do not have to cheat or lie to get a blessing. Trust God in your choices and directions you take and you do not have to hide from any man on how you were blessed.

> "You shall not steal, nor deal falsely, nor lie to one another. And you shall not swear by My name falsely, nor shall you profane the name of your God: I *am* the Lord. You shall not cheat your neighbor, nor rob *him*. The wages of him who is hired shall not remain with you all night until morning."
>
> Leviticus 19:11-13 (NKJV)

Having the right friends will help you get to where God wants you to go. The wrong friends can keep you or slow you from getting to your intended destination. In order to have the right friends, there are risks you have to take.

There are four kinds of risks involved in being a good friend:

1. Intellectual

    a. You have to read things you do not normally read.

    b. You have to listen to people or friends that can challenge you.

2. Physical

    a. You have to push your limit. You must be willing to do things (legal things only) for friends when they need you. This might mean getting out of your bed in the middle of the night to console them.

3. Emotional

    a. Learn to meet new people.

    b. Allow a friend to see a side of you never seen before.

4. Spiritual

    a. Do not let the devil shut your mouth. If the Lord has a word for you to share with a friend or others, then you should share that word. Of course, those people will have to act upon whatever the Lord leads them to do and not just because you said it.

There are always risks in friendships that include disclosing your vulnerabilities. These vulnerabilities will include personal weaknesses and shortcomings. A true friend will be able to show himself or herself for who they really are, even at the chance of being corrected by the friend. If you have some character flaws or personality issues, then the friend should be able to point them out and help you become a better person.

Do not be afraid to make a choice, but never make a choice without considering options and consequences. Never make a choice just because everyone else is doing it. If that close friend is doing something you know is not right and God is warning you about the issue, do not be disobedient to God!

You should always move in positive directions that are in your mind. If your friend is more progressive in life than you, do not allow jealously to step in. Use this information to inspire you to do better things than you are currently doing. Do not make these choices to compete with your friend, but to improve your own personal life or situation. God has a plan for your life that includes an abundance of blessings, including good friends.

> I call heaven and earth as witnesses today against you, *that* I have set before you life and death, blessing and cursing; therefore choose life, that both you and your descendants may live; that you may love the LORD your God, that you may obey His voice, and that you may cling to Him, for He *is* your life and the length of your days; and that you may dwell in the land which the LORD swore to your fathers, to Abraham, Isaac, and Jacob, to give them.
>
> Deuteronomy 30:19-20 (NKJV)

When having to choose the lesser of two evils, choose neither. Christians should upgrade their environments. This includes choosing better friends and getting involved in positive things. Learn to do more than what is required. You should learn to add value to something you already have. No matter your situation or circumstances, God has the power to do anything great; especially things once thought impossible!

Singer/group Israel Houghton and New Breed

sang a song called, "I'm a Friend of God." You should see God as your friend, whom you can talk to about anything. God should be able to call you friend for seeking and doing his will and doing what he would have you do. God will be a friend to you when your earthly friends cannot or will not be there for you.

And the LORD said: "I have surely seen the oppression of My people who *are* in Egypt, and have heard their cry because of their taskmasters, for I know their sorrows. So I have come down to deliver them out of the hand of the Egyptians, and to bring them up from that land to a good and large land, to a land flowing with milk and honey, to the place of the Canaanites and the Hittites and the Amorites and the Perizzites and the Hivites and the Jebusites. Now therefore, behold, the cry of the children of Israel has come to Me, and I have also seen the oppression with which the Egyptians oppress them. Come now, therefore, and I will send you to Pharaoh that you may bring My people, the children of Israel, out of Egypt." But Moses said to God, "Who *am* I that I should go to Pharaoh, and that I should bring the children of Israel out of Egypt?" So He said, "I will certainly be with you. And this *shall be* a sign to you that I have sent you:

When you have brought the people out of Egypt,
you shall serve God on this mountain."

Exodus 3:7-12 (NKJV)

Let God continue to work on you. God uses people who are industrious and not lazy. Do not try to understand every little thing that God will have you do. Let go of the importance of needing to understand what God is doing. Some of the best and most respected ministers today did not initially intend to become preachers. They went through some things in their lives and God called on them to do something they were not expecting—to preach his word! Experience has shown that God will tell you to do something that seemed virtually impossible; however, should you follow his word, you will never fail!

Always know who you are. "I am" tells me who I am. Do not let anybody tell you who you are. If you are under construction, do not establish friendship with someone with mutual dislikes. This kind of relationship usually breeds negativity. Do not be afraid to make positive personal changes in your life. When God is finished with you, you will be like gold.

Making friends is good, but sometimes, no matter how hard you try, some people will hate you. Sometimes those you call "friend" will become envious of you when God blesses you. Do not let this bother you. Remember, the bigger your enemy, the bigger the blessing. Always believe God will bless you with what you need.

God's Word will not be mocked. Whatever God says he will do, he will do! Do not be in a hurry to make friends with just about anybody. You should be friendly to everyone, but not everyone needs to be your close friend. Let God show you with whom you should spend quality time.

"Now therefore, speak to the men of Judah and to the inhabitants of Jerusalem, saying, 'Thus says the LORD: "Behold, I am fashioning a disaster and devising a plan against you. Return now every one from his evil way, and make your ways and your doings good." And they said, "That is hopeless! So we will walk according to our own plans, and we will every one obey the dictates of his evil heart." Therefore thus says the LORD: "Ask now among the Gentiles, who has heard such things? The virgin of Israel has done a very horrible thing. Will *a man* leave the snow water of Lebanon, *which comes* from the rock of the field? Will the cold flowing waters be forsaken for strange waters? "Because My people have forgotten Me, they have burned incense to worthless idols. And they have caused themselves to stumble in their ways, *from* the ancient paths, to walk in pathways and not on a highway.

Jeremiah 18:11-15 (NKJV)

Surely you have things turned around! Shall the potter be esteemed as the clay; For shall the thing made say of him who made it, "He did not make me"? Or shall the thing formed say of him who formed it, "He has no understanding"? *Is* it not yet a very little while till Lebanon shall be turned into a fruitful field, and the fruitful field be esteemed as a forest? In that day the deaf shall hear the words of the book, and the eyes of the blind shall see out of obscurity and out of darkness. The humble also shall increase *their* joy in the LORD, and the poor among men shall rejoice in the Holy One of Israel. For the terrible one is brought to nothing, the scornful one is consumed, and all who watch for iniquity are cut off. Who makes a man an offender by a word, and lay a snare for him who reproves in the gate, and turn aside the just by empty words.

Isaiah 29:16-21 (NKJV)

God is the owner of everything on earth. He has the power to bless you with whatever he wants. Many people believe we should only pray for our needs, but not our wants. God knows our needs and our wants. He is capable and willing to provide both.

> The earth *is* the LORD's, and all its fullness, the world and those who dwell therein. For He has founded it upon the seas, and established it upon the waters.
>
> Psalms 24:1-2 (NKJV)

Whatever you want, wants you. This includes friends. If you want good friends, there are folks out there that want you as a friend. Seek God first, and all the rest will be added unto you. Personal relationships should never overshadow your relationship with God. Your relationship with God should be first, and above everything else!

Do not be afraid of having to go through problems. Talk to the Lord first. If you have a personal relationship with the Lord, he will guide you. There is an advantage to having a good Christian friend to talk to about things that are on your mind, even if it is just a sanity check on your proposed solution to problems. You know that God is in your life when you go through something and you survive it.

dreams

Everybody must have a dream for his or her life. Life without chasing dreams or reaching goals is meaningless. A good Christian friend can be rewarding in our daily growth. A good friend will be happy to see you reach for and achieve your dreams. You should seek God's will at all times.

> Blessed *is* the man who walks not in the counsel of the ungodly, nor stands in the path of sinners, nor sits in the seat of the scornful; But his delight *is* in the law of the LORD, and in His law he meditates day and night. He shall be like a tree planted by the rivers of water, that brings forth its fruit in its season, whose leaf also shall not wither; and whatever he does shall prosper.
>
> Psalms 1:1-3 (NKJV)

Now to Him who is able to do exceedingly abundantly above all that we ask or think, according to the power that works in us, to Him *be* glory in the church by Christ Jesus to all generations, forever and ever. Amen. I, therefore, the prisoner of the Lord, beseech you to walk worthy of the calling with which you were called.

Ephesians 3:20-4:1 (NKJV)

There are different kinds of dreamers. There are those that have no dreams at all, and then there are those that acknowledge God-given dreams. While paying attention to your dreams, you should attempt great things that God has placed in your heart and soul to do. You must beware of the dream busters: family, friends, failure, fatigue, and fear. These people and things can be distractions from what God will have you do in your life. You must overcome all these obstacles.

Therefore we do not lose heart. Even though our outward man is perishing, yet the inward *man* is being renewed day by day. For our light affliction, which is but for a moment, is working for us a far more exceeding *and* eternal weight of glory, while we do not look at the things which are seen, but at the things which are not seen. For the things which are seen *are* temporary, but the things which are not seen *are* eternal.

2 Corinthians 4:16-18 (NKJV)

Failure in life is sometimes there to make you stronger. Sometimes the failure will be in the relationships with our friends. When certain friendships fail or become unfruitful, do not be afraid of moving forward. You should be more afraid of standing still. Some friends are meant for a season, and others are meant for a lifetime.

Since you seek a proof of Christ speaking in me, who is not weak toward you, but mighty in you. For though He was crucified in weakness, yet He lives by the power of God. For we also are weak in Him, but we shall live with Him by the power of God toward you. Examine yourselves *as to* whether you are in the faith. Test yourselves. Do you not know yourselves, that Jesus Christ is in you?—unless indeed you are disqualified. But I trust that you will know that we are not disqualified. Now I pray to God that you do no evil, not that we should appear approved, but that you should do what is honorable, though we may seem disqualified. For we can do nothing against the truth, but for the truth. For we are glad when we are weak and you are strong. And this also we pray, that you may be made complete. Therefore I write these things being absent, lest being present I should use sharpness, according to the authority which the Lord

> has given me for edification and not for destruc-
> tion. Finally, brethren, farewell. Become complete.
> Be of good comfort, be of one mind, live in peace;
> and the God of love and peace will be with you.
> Greet one another with a holy kiss. All the saints
> greet you.
>
> 2 Corinthians 13:3-13 (NKJV)

Love is one of the most important gifts God gives us
in life. The first bit of love you are normally aware of
is love from family. You should realize that God has
loved you even before you were born! The next level
of love often comes from friends. The most excellent
quality of life is love. The best way to teach another
person love is to show them love. You should ask yourself: do you love on the right level? The Bible teaches
us to love not only our friends, but our enemies as
well. We should show love to all, but we should show
a special love to our friends and family.

> "You have heard that it was said, '*You shall love
> your neighbor* and hate your enemy.' But I say to
> you, love your enemies, bless those who curse you,
> do good to those who hate you, and pray for those
> who spitefully use you and persecute you, that
> you may be sons of your Father in heaven; for He
> makes His sun rise on the evil and on the good,

and sends rain on the just and on the unjust. For if you love those who love you, what reward have you? Do not even the tax collectors do the same? And if you greet your brethren only, what do you do more *than others?* Do not even the tax collectors do so? Therefore you shall be perfect, just as your Father in heaven is perfect. Take heed that you do not do your charitable deeds before men, to be seen by them. Otherwise you have no reward from your Father in heaven."

Matthew 5:43-6:1 (NKJV)

As in any relationship, there are difficulties in friendship. To keep a relationship going, sometimes you should take the blame when it is not your fault. As a friend, you should display undeserved generosity, and show patience with slow, unconditional commitment. Sometimes you have to give underserved friendship. You should stand for the poor, weak, and defenseless.

In friendship, you should be forgiving and give respect for authority. True friends will provide cheerful generosity and show love in correction. A true friend would not want you for just what you could do for them. A true friend will also seek to find what you need from them as a friend.

friendship at a higher level

> By night on my bed I sought the one I love; I sought him, but I did not find him. "I will rise now," *I said*, "And go about the city; in the streets and in the squares I will seek the one I love." I sought him, but I did not find him. The watchmen who go about the city found me; *I said*, "Have you seen the one I love?" Scarcely had I passed by them, when I found the one I love. I held him and would not let him go, until I had brought him to the house of my mother, and into the chamber of her who conceived me. I charge you, O daughters of Jerusalem, by the gazelles or by the does of the field, do not stir up nor awaken love until it pleases.
>
> Song of Songs 3:1-5 (NKJV)

There are some things that only God can accomplish. You should only turn to God for approval of whom you should have as a mate. Keep in mind, no romantic or sensual relationship with another human being will satisfy craving in the flesh. The craving will just intensify until you lose control. God is the only person people should lust after.

This is especially true since our friends and mates will sometimes let us down. A male Christian friend recently discussed how he prayed for a mate and met a nice Christian woman. He tried to do all the right things, including not having sex before marriage, making sure his fiancée was a Christian and not just a believer, and receiving marriage counseling. However, after getting married and facing a host of financial commitments with his new wife, she decided she could not live with her new life, including moving to a new state due to the man's job move. She filed for divorce. This could have been devastating for some, but the friend realized his trust and faith in God is more important than placing blame on God for his situation.

> I spread out my hands to You; My soul *longs* for You like a thirsty land. *Selah* answer me speedily, O LORD; My spirit fails! Do not hide Your face from me, lest I be like those who go down into the pit. Cause me to hear Your lovingkindness in

the morning, for in You do I trust; Cause me to know the way in which I should walk, For I lift up my soul to You. Deliver me, O LORD, from my enemies; In You I take shelter. Teach me to do Your will, For You *are* my God; Your Spirit *is* good. Lead me in the land of uprightness.

Psalms 143:6-10 (NKJV)

There is some sanity in the saying that our spouses should be our best friend. However, this may not always be the case. All intimate relationships with the opposite sex should be based on a friendship first. We must be careful with whom we become intimate. Real intimacy is a journey into the unknown. It adds new dimension to life. Commitment and loyalty are a part of love.

Beware! We must close the door to anything that may cause us to stop loving God. If the person you are considering becoming intimate with wants to pull you from your relationship with God, slow down, evaluate the situation, and pray that God shows you what to do with this person. If God is leading you away from this person, do not be afraid that you will not be able to meet someone else.

O God, You *are* my God; Early will I seek You; My soul thirsts for You; My flesh longs for You in a dry and thirsty land where there is no water. So I have looked for You in the sanctuary, to see Your power and Your glory. Because Your loving kindness *is* better than life, my lips shall praise You. Thus I will bless You while I live; I will lift up my hands in Your name. My soul shall be satisfied as with marrow and fatness, and my mouth shall praise You with joyful lips. When I remember You on my bed, I meditate on You in the *night* watches. Because You have been my help, therefore in the shadow of Your wings I will rejoice. My soul follows close behind You; Your right hand upholds me.

Psalms 63:1-8 (NKJV)

All serious dating relationships should lead to marriage. Anything below that is a waste of your time. Keep in mind we are talking about dating, and not about being platonic friends. There should be no time limit or higher-level relationship expectations in platonic friends.

Author Emily Seate wrote in *"A True Friend"* (Seate)[1] that you should value honesty and respect in your relationship. She also said that friendship requires investment, and friends have to willingly and gladly invest in each other. Christians should seek to find and enjoy friendships with like-minded individuals. This should enhance a Christian's personal life and servitude to the Lord.

God created us all with a need to have friends. As mentioned earlier, it has been said that your spouse should be your best friend. Relationship expert Jimmy Evans described friendship as a "fundamental need" of the human heart (Evans)[2]. Evans said that friendship is hard to find due to our culture's push to immediately sexualize a relationship between a man and a woman. We agree with Evans in that sexual relationships that occur very early in a dating relationship prevent true friendship from ever developing. Premarital sex can cause an emotional stunting of the relationship.

Evans provided solutions to when you don't have friendship in marriage: being faithful, believing in one another, and embracing your differences. In being faithful, Evans said that with every great friend there is always a positive history, i.e. a string of sacrifices and choices each of you made for each other and for your relationship. We agree that without that history, there is no meaningful friendship. Proverbs 17:17 tells us that "a friend loves at all times, and a brother is born for adversity." Evans said that if you're going to make your wife or your husband your best friend, you will have to commit yourself to being faithful to them.

You can't consider someone your best friend if they don't believe in you. Evans said that our spouses need to see our belief in them. We can't put our spouses down and think that we can build a strong friendship. We agree that friends believe in one another. In Christian friendships and in marriage, there are times when we're going to need to be able to speak into each other's lives. There will be issues that we need to deal with and corrective things we need to say to each other. But this will require a foundation of firm belief in one another, especially in marriage.

Evans said that friends celebrate their differences by embracing their differences. Differences can be either dangerous or dynamic in relationships. The outcome will depend on how we choose to respond to the differences with our spouses. Best friends will look at each other appreciatively and acknowledge how they complement one another. They should be able to count on the other's strengths and support them through their weaknesses.

conclusion

At the completion of this book, the authors had been friends for over twenty-eight years. They met while each served in the U.S. Air Force, on their way to separate remote tours in Alaska. They remained friends through occasional contact by phone and sporadic in-person visits when assignment locations and business trips to another's living location would allow. Dr. Wilson, though not always living accordingly in the early years, was a Christian during the whole time. He would occasionally talk to Joyce about the Lord, but she did not want to hear it, and did what she wanted to do. She eventually found the Lord on her own, and that brought the friends closer. She has been and is now a strong prayer warrior with Dr. Wilson in dealing with life's problems. They both were single when they met, but each got married to others during the friendship. God has blessed them to remain friends through a failed first marriage for Dr. Wilson, and later the death of Joyce's husband.

While Joyce's husband was alive, he accepted the

fact that Dr. Wilson and Joyce were just friends and did not feel threatened by it. The friendship never caused any problems in Joyce's marriage. Dr. Wilson's current wife of twenty-one years is fully aware of the ongoing friendship and does not feel threatened. Most problems come from friends or family who do not understand how anyone could have a friend of the opposite sex outside of marriage and not be sleeping with them. We feel most of this suspicion is based on these persons' own insecurities and weaknesses.

God will place people in your life for many different reasons. God places some folks in your life so they can be a help or support for you for a season or a lifetime. God places other people in your life so you could be a help to them or speak God's Word into their lives. Many relationships are mutually beneficial to both parties. Whatever the reason, seek God's counsel on what he will have to do with or say to a friend. If you seek his will, God will place the right words to say in your mouth and lead you to do the right things. Never place a limit on what God can do in your life, and do not be afraid to show yourself to the people that God places in your life.

references

1 Emily Seate; A True Friend; http://www.ezinearti-
   cles.com/?A-True-Friend&id=733755; 19 Sep 2007

2 Evans, Jimmy; Our Secret Paradise; pp. 109-116;
   Regal Books; Ventura, 2006